CW00848053

This book was presented to

_____

on the occasion of

_____

date

_____

BIBLE
Questions
& Answers

written by Marjorie Newman
illustrated by Michael Codd

World
HORIZONS

Designed by Ian Gwilt.

Copyright © 1991 World International Publishing Limited.
Published in Great Britain by World International Publishing Limited,
An Egmont Company, Egmont House, PO Box 111,
Great Ducie Street, Manchester M60 3BL.
World Horizons is an imprint of World International Publishing Limited.
All rights reserved. No part of this publication may be reproduced,
stored in a retrieval system, or transmitted, in any form or by any means,
electronic, mechanical, photocopying, recording or otherwise, without
prior permission of the copyright owners.

Printed in Malaysia.

British Library Cataloguing in Publication Data
Newman, Marjorie.
    Bible questions and answers.
    1. Christianity. Scriptures
    I. Title II. Codd, Michael, 1938 –
220

ISBN 0-7498-0318-5

Introduction

I certainly learned a great deal while working on these Bible questions and answers! I had never before visualized clearly the incredible distances which Bible people travelled, the hardships under which they lived, or the amazing skills which they developed.

It was a difficult book to write in so far as we don't really know some of the answers. They are not all hard facts. Sometimes we need to look at the evidence and make up our own minds.

I used the Bible as my main source of reference; but some of the questions required me to look at other historical texts. The questions are arranged in subject order rather than chronologically, since this seemed the better way.

For me, the more we discover about the Bible the more fascinating it becomes. I hope you will feel the same! Perhaps you will read this book, then go on to make further explorations of your own.

Marjorie Newman

Contents

The Holy Book

Why is the Bible special?

Christians believe that the Bible is God's word. It tells us who He is, what He has done, and what He will do in the future. It tells us why the world is the way it is, and what His plans for it are. It tells us about Heaven. It contains promises and warnings. And it is meant for everyone in the world.

God can talk to us through His book. It is *very* special.

Is the Bible just one book?

Not really. It is a collection of books, written by many different people. But all the books help us to understand more about God.

Do we know who wrote the books of the Bible?

We know who wrote most of them. The books are divided into two main sets, called the Old Testament and the New Testament.

Some of the Old Testament writings are so old we don't know exactly who wrote them down in the first place. Time after time, as the manuscripts wore out, scribes carefully made new copies. It is possible that the scribe Ezra (whose story is in the Bible) collected and arranged many of the books of the Old Testament.

We know the names of the writers of the New Testament because – except for the writer of Hebrews – we can find them in the Bible. The first four books were written by Matthew, Mark, Luke and John, and are known as the Gospels, or 'Good News'.

How many books are there in the Bible?

Basically there are 39 books in the Old Testament and all Bibles have the same 27 books in the New Testament.

How many words are there in the Bible?

Counting the Bible as 66 books, there are 929 chapters in the Old Testament, and 260 in the New. The Old Testament has 23,214 verses, and 592,439 words. The New Testament has 7,959 verses and 181,253 words. (Perhaps you'll check to see if this is right!)

How did the Bible come to be written?

The scribes wrote down the stories and facts so that they would be remembered correctly. The Old Testament contains the story of how God created the world; the history of the Jewish nation; God's instructions on how to live and the sayings of many wise men.

The New Testament was written to tell people of the life and teaching of Jesus Christ, and of the things which happened to the early Christians. It also contains many epistles, or letters.

Luke says he wrote his gospel so that his friend Theophilus would know that the stories which he had been hearing about Jesus were true – Luke had investigated them very carefully (Luke 1: 1–4).

But all the books were 'inspired' by God. That is, the authors were guided by God so it was as if God Himself was writing them.

Why do some of the stories vary in details?

The people who wrote them put down what they had seen, or been told. We can understand these differences better if, when something exciting has happened, we try asking three or four different people who were there at the time what they saw and heard. They will probably all say slightly different things.

How were the books of the New Testament collected together?

When the early Christians met together they would have had readings from the Old Testament, just as they

What language was the Bible written in?

The Old Testament was written in Hebrew and Aramaic, which looks like this

ויגברו המים

The New Testament was written in Greek, which looks like this

Στην αρχή
ήταν ο λόγος

How soon was the Bible translated into other languages?

We know that there was a Greek translation of the Old Testament, known as the Septuagint, which was begun in the third century BC.

Translation of the New Testament began almost as soon as it was completed. Its first translation was probably into Latin, because this was the official language of the Roman Empire, although the early Christians spoke Greek.

were accustomed to in the Synagogue. But they would also have had stories about Jesus, and His teaching; and they are most probably the people who chose exactly which of these books should be included in the New Testament.

Who was Jerome, and why is he important?

In AD 384, Jerome was secretary to Pope Damasus. Until then, there had been various translations of the Bible. People began to feel they should have just one version. So Pope Damasus asked Jerome to write one. Jerome took the trouble to go and live in Bethlehem for many years and learn Hebrew, so that he could read the original texts. His Latin translation is known as the Vulgate.

Many other translations have since been made, based on Jerome's version. Among them were the first translations into English.

How many languages has the Bible been translated into now?

The Bible (both Old and New Testaments, or New Testament only) has been translated into over 586 languages. Bible translators are working all the time to add to them. Sometimes, Christians working for this purpose have been the first people to write a language down at all.

How long did it take to write the Bible?

It took many hundreds of years.

Who was John Wycliffe?

John Wycliffe was an Englishman. He lived in the 14th century, mostly during the reign of King Edward the Third. Until then the Latin Bible had been used in England. It was read out in the churches; but only the learned people could understand it. John thought the Bible was so important everyone should be able to hear it (and read it) in their own language.

Because of him, by 1384 the Vulgate had been translated into English; although John Purvey, Nicholas of Heresford, and some others did most of the actual translating.

At first the text read very strangely! The translators had been so keen to get everything accurate they had kept much of the order of the Latin words. But by only eleven years later John Purvey had written a clearer version.

In 1934, a society called the Wycliffe Bible Translators was formed. The members still work on Bible translations today.

Why are there different 'versions' of the Bible?

Because the English language has changed so much over the centuries, certain scholars have at different times in history produced updated versions of the Bible which contained a more modern use of the English language. For example, the phrase 'After this manner therefore pray ye' in a Bible written in 1611 is rewritten as 'This is the way you should pray' in a modern translation.

Another reason is that some versions of the Bible are direct and highly accurate translations of ancient Hebrew and Greek manuscripts whereas others are simplified or 'paraphrased' versions.

How many books of the Bible were written by Paul?

Thirteen. They were written as letters to the people of the churches he had started on his missionary journeys.

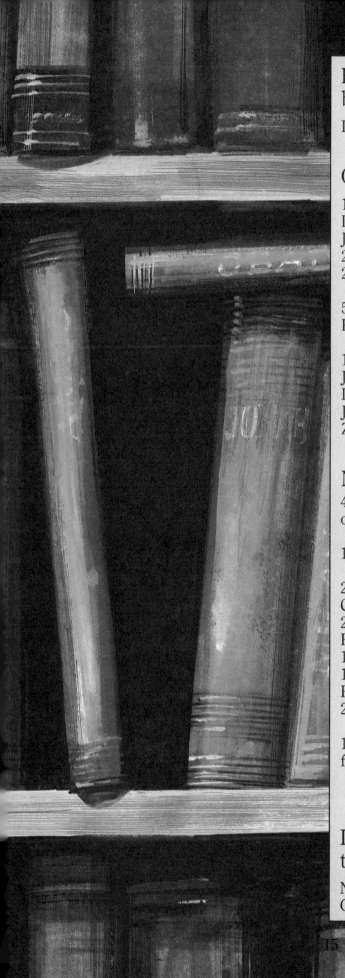

How might we divide up the books of the Bible?

It has often been done this way:

Old Testament

17 History books: Genesis, Exodus, Leviticus, Numbers, Deuteronomy, Joshua, Judges, Ruth, 1 Samuel, 2 Samuel, 1 Kings, 2 Kings, 1 Chronicles, 2 Chronicles, Ezra, Nehemiah, Esther

5 Poetical books: Job, Psalms, Proverbs, Ecclesiastes, Song of Songs

17 Books of the Prophets: Isaiah, Jeremiah, Lamentations, Ezekiel, Daniel, Hosea, Joel, Amos, Obadiah, Jonah, Micah, Nahum, Habakkuk, Zephaniah, Haggai, Zechariah, Malachi

New Testament

4 Books telling the story of Jesus' life on earth: Matthew, Mark, Luke, John

1 History book: Acts

21 Books of teaching about Jesus and Christianity: Romans, 1 Corinthians, 2 Corinthians, Galatians, Ephesians, Philippians, Colossians, 1 Thessalonians, 2 Thessalonians, 1 Timothy, 2 Timothy, Titus, Philemon, Hebrews, James, 1 Peter, 2 Peter, 1 John, 2 John, 3 John, Jude

1 Book which speaks mostly of the future: Revelation

Is the Bible still being added to?

No. It is complete. Everything which God wanted to say in it has been said.

Bible Lands

Can we be sure where most of the Bible stories took place?

We know for certain that most of the Bible stories took place in a narrow area at the eastern end of the Mediterranean Sea; but we can't be sure about all the exact locations.

Jerusalem is on the same site as it always was. So are Bethlehem and Nazareth.

Was the Red Sea in the Bible the same one as today's Red Sea?

The story about the Red Sea, in Exodus 14, is very exciting. The Israelites were escaping from slavery in Egypt. God wanted the Egyptians to learn He was truly God. As the Israelites reached the edge of the desert, God told Moses to lead them back towards a place called Pi Hahrioth. They were to camp there, between Migdol and the sea. The Egyptians would think the Israelites were confused and lost, and come after them to recapture them.

Near nightfall, the Israelites saw the Egyptian army in the distance. Moses prayed urgently to God. And God said, "Tell the people to move forward." Move forward? That would mean walking into the Red Sea!

But the Israelites did move forward. God told Moses to stretch out his rod over the waters. Moses obeyed. The sea divided; and the amazed Israelites walked across. But in the morning, when the Egyptians tried to follow, God told Moses to hold out his rod again. The waters came crashing down. Every one of the Egyptians was drowned; and every one of the Israelites was saved.

Most Bible scholars think that what we call the Red Sea today is not the same one; but they can't agree where the original Red Sea was. Many people think the story referred to the depression known as the Bitter Lakes, near today's Suez. The Suez gulf may have extended further north than it does now.

The Bible name 'Red Sea' could be translated more accurately as 'The Sea of Reeds'.

Is Mount Sinai the same?

We are not sure. Since the 4th century BC, Mount Sinai (also known as Horeb) has been placed in the mountainous southern region of the Peninsula of Sinai, between the two arms of the Red Sea. But in Exodus 19 verse 18, the Bible says smoke billowed up from the mountain like smoke from a furnace. Some people think this means that Mount Sinai was in a volcanic area, possibly north-west Arabia. This would have placed it in Midianite territory, and fits in with the story of Moses and the burning bush (Exodus 3: 1, 2). However, unless it was in Edomite territory it would not fit in with Elijah's journey of 41 days from Beersheba (1 Kings 19: 3–9).

Is it important to pinpoint the exact locations?

No. The significance or meaning of the stories is far more important.

Through the centuries man has changed the names of all sorts of towns, cities and other types of places. For example, the country of Abyssinia changed its name to Ethiopia. In the same way, some of the places in the Bible have had their names changed also. This means that we cannot always be certain where all the places in the Bible actually are.

SEA OF GALILEE

River Jordan

Bethlehem

DEAD SEA

EDOM

How big was the Promised Land?

The 'Promised Land' was quite small. The Bible says it stretched 'from Dan to Beersheba', which means it was about 240 kilometres long from north to south. From east to west it averaged about 80 kilometres. The land was shaped rather like a crescent between the desert and the sea.

From the sea this area of land rises up to a height of about 1,000 metres, then descends into the Jordan valley. It rises again on the eastern side of the valley, reaching a height of about 2,000 metres in Edom, and over 3,000 metres around the region of Mount Hermon.

Where did Jesus live?

Until He began His work of telling
people about the Kingdom of God,
Jesus lived in Galilee, a northern
region of the land of Palestine. He was
born in Bethlehem of Judea, in the
south; and He did much of His
teaching in the southern region.

What was the climate like?

The climate would have been the same
as it is in that region today. In summer
the temperature in Upper Galilee
reaches 22 degrees centigrade while
around Jericho it can reach the upper
thirties to forties. The yearly rainfall
may be up to 152 centimetres in the
Hermon area, and only 10 centimetres
in the Jordan valley.

The winds can be dramatic. The
east wind is relentlessly hot and
drying, while the west wind often
brings devastating storms.

Was it difficult to survive in
the desert of the Bible lands?

It was very difficult. People had to be
taught which cactus they could get
water from, and how to collect wild
honey.

When the Israelites were wandering
in the desert on their way to the
Promised Land they became afraid
they would starve. But God sent food
to them in the form of manna, or
'bread from Heaven', which they had
to pick up from the ground each
morning. He also sent flocks of quails
– small birds – which they could kill
and eat for meat every evening
(Exodus 16: 2–17).

The Bible says that John the Baptist
ate locusts in the desert. But this
probably means locust beans from the
carob tree, rather than the insects
(Mark 1: 6)! Carob is still used today as
a substitute for chocolate.

Is there archaeological evidence for the fall of Jericho?

Yes. Archaeologist Dr John Garstang, director of the British School of Archaeology in Jerusalem and of the Department of Antiquities of the Palestine Government, excavated the ruins of Jericho from 1929 to 1936; and in the 1950s Dame Kathleen Kenyon, a British archaeologist, also excavated there. They found evidence that the fall of Jericho did happen at the time of Joshua, and that the walls did actually 'fall down flat', as some translations of the Bible say (Joshua 6: 20). The walls were built on uneven foundations. The foundations are still there, tilting outwards!

Dr Garstang found that the walls had been double, about three metres apart, linked together by building

houses across the top – just as the Bible says of Rahab's house. Rahab was the lady who hid Joshua's spies on her roof. When it was safe, she let down a rope from her outside window so that the spies could slide down it and escape to safety. In return they promised that she and her household should not be harmed in the attack which was to come. The promise was kept (Joshua 2: 1–24).

Once the walls had fallen, God had told Joshua to destroy Jericho by burning it to the ground. Dr Garstang found a thick layer of ashes left by a huge fire. Underneath it, turned into charcoal, were wheat, barley, dates and other foods; possibly evidence of another of God's commands – that Joshua's army should not take for themselves any goods which they found in Jericho.

Have archaeologists made other interesting discoveries in the Bible lands?

Many interesting discoveries have been made. Here are two!

When the Israelites were slaves in Egypt, they were forced to make bricks. In order to make the work harder for them, Pharaoh commanded that they no longer be supplied with the straw which was one of the ingredients of brick-making. They would have to find their own (Exodus 5: 7–9). (We still talk about 'trying to make bricks without straw' to describe a difficult or impossible task.)

In Exodus 1 verse 14, the Bible mentions Pithom as one of the places where these bricks were made. Archaeologists Naville (in 1883) and Kyle (in 1908) excavated the site. They found that the lower bricks in the buildings had a good amount of chopped straw in them; the middle bricks had much less straw; and the top bricks had no straw at all!

On the site of the city of Ur (where Abraham lived) Woolley, another archaeologist, discovered the ruins of a schoolroom. He found stone tablets on which were written exercises in mathematics, grammar, history and medicine. This may have been the school which Abraham went to as a boy!

Are the places mentioned in Paul's journeys accurate?

Yes. It's only the exact routes that are difficult to place.

Paul made three great missionary journeys – journeys to tell people about Jesus, and encourage them to become Christians.

His first journey was to Galatia. Paul and his companions Barnabas and John Mark started out from Antioch. The region of Galatia in Asia Minor was about 480 kilometres to the north-west. They travelled via Cyprus. When they reached Pamphylia John Mark deserted them, and went home.

Paul and Barnabas travelled on. They reached another Antioch – Antioch of Pisidia. There Paul gave his message. He spoke first to the Jews; but the Gentiles (non-Jews) also wanted to hear him. So Paul preached to them also. Furious Jews made trouble for Paul and Barnabas; so the two travelled on, going 160 kilometres east to Iconium.

The same sort of thing happened again. This time Paul and Barnabas travelled on to Lystra, about 32 kilometres south of Iconium; then to Derbe, 48 kilometres to the south-east of Lystra.

At Lystra a mob of people turned against the two. Barnabas escaped; but Paul was stoned. He wasn't killed, and Barnabas bravely returned to Lystra to find him. However, it was time for them to move on again. They retraced their steps, travelling via Lystra, Iconium and Antioch back to the Antioch from which they had set out (Acts 13, 14).

Paul's second missionary journey was to Greece. This time Silas went with him. Travelling via Lystra, Paul met Timothy, and Timothy also accompanied him from then on.

It seems Paul thought he should go to Ephesus; but God stopped him. So he started to go north into Bithynia. Again God stopped him. Paul then went north-west to Troas. At Troas Luke joined them, travelling with them to Philippi. There Luke stayed, not joining Paul again until six years later (Acts 20: 6 – when Luke changes 'they' back to 'we').

Philippi, on the north-east corner of Greece, was where Paul started the first church in Europe.

Paul and Silas travelled on, going 160 kilometres west to Thessalonica in Macedonia. After a short time they moved to Berea, then to Athens, the Greek capital. From Athens they went to Corinth, where they stayed for a year and a half. They then returned to Jerusalem and Antioch; but on the way Paul was able to stop at Ephesus, which he had long wanted to visit (Acts 15: 36 to 18: 22).

Paul's third missionary journey was to Ephesus. From Ephesus he went again to Greece, visiting Corinth, going through Macedonia, and sailing from Philippi.

Paul's journeys took about twelve years altogether, from AD45 to 57. When they ended the Christian message had been told in almost every city of Asia Minor and Greece – the centre of the then-known world.

Perhaps you will travel to the Bible lands one day. Or maybe you already have!

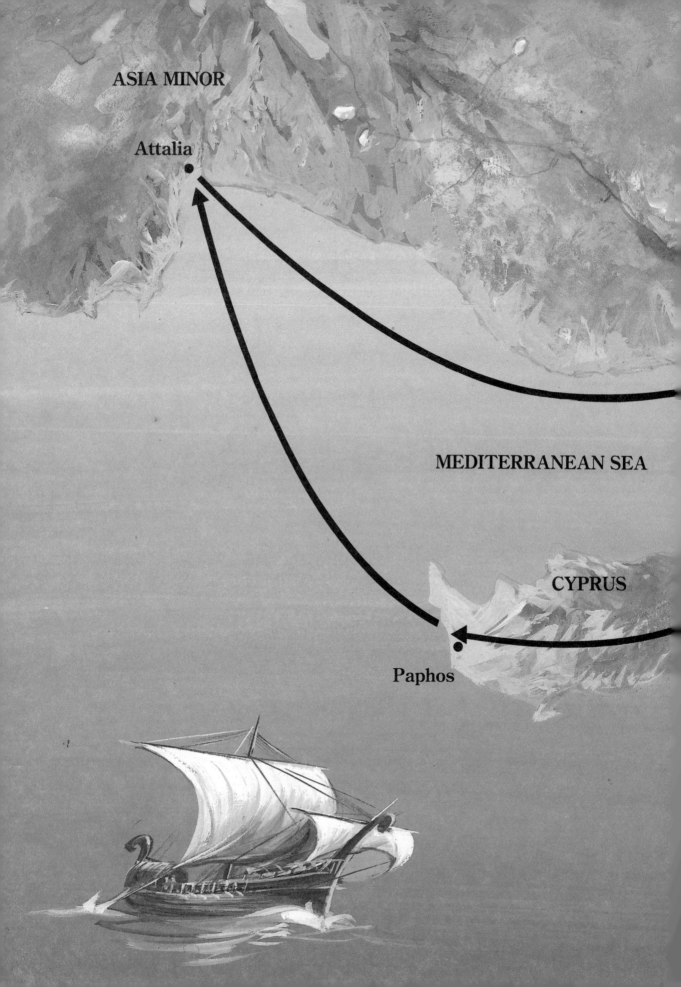

ASIA MINOR

Attalia

MEDITERRANEAN SEA

CYPRUS

Paphos

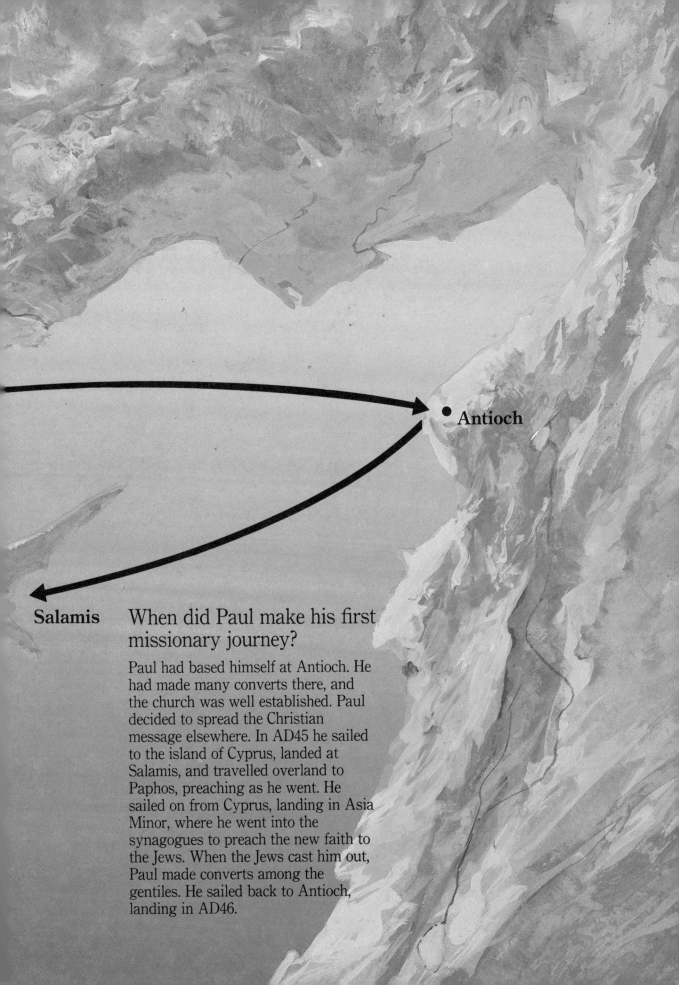

Antioch

Salamis

When did Paul make his first missionary journey?

Paul had based himself at Antioch. He had made many converts there, and the church was well established. Paul decided to spread the Christian message elsewhere. In AD45 he sailed to the island of Cyprus, landed at Salamis, and travelled overland to Paphos, preaching as he went. He sailed on from Cyprus, landing in Asia Minor, where he went into the synagogues to preach the new faith to the Jews. When the Jews cast him out, Paul made converts among the gentiles. He sailed back to Antioch, landing in AD46.

Leaders

Did Abraham really live to be 175 years old?

This is what the Bible says. God certainly blessed Abraham with a very long life.

Abraham's wife Sarah is recorded as having lived to be 127, and one of his sons, Ishmael, to be 137 (Genesis 23: 1; 25: 7, 17).

Who was chosen by God to be the leader of the Israelites?

God chose Moses to lead the Israelites out of Egypt, where they were being cruelly treated as slaves.

Moses was an Israelite himself; but he wasn't a slave, as the others were. He had been brought up in the palace by the Princess, daughter of the Egyptian Pharaoh.

One day, angry at seeing an Israelite slave mistreated, Moses killed the Egyptian task-master and fled to Midian. When God told him he was to go back to Egypt to speak to the Pharaoh and demand the release of the slaves, Moses was very much afraid. He even argued with God about it.

But in the end he obeyed, reassured that God would be with him. He did lead the people out of Egypt, and remained their leader for the forty years they wandered in the desert on their journey to the Promised Land (Exodus chapters 1–12 for the beginning of the story and the escape from Egypt. Other chapters in Exodus and Numbers for the desert story).

Did Moses enter the Promised Land?

As they journeyed through the desert the Israelites continually grumbled, and doubted God. Even when they were very close to the Promised Land they still didn't trust Him.

Acting on God's orders, Moses sent twelve men to spy out the land of Canaan before the Israelite attack. When ten of the spies reported that the

Canaanites were as huge as giants, and their cities like fortresses, the Israelites panicked. "It would have been better if we'd died in Egypt!" they cried. They refused to pay attention to Joshua and Caleb, the other two spies. When Joshua and Caleb reminded them that the Canaanites had no protection which could match the power of God, the Israelites picked up stones, ready to stone them to death.

But God appeared at the tabernacle in a cloud of glory, so that all the Israelites could see His majesty. He spoke to Moses. "How long will these people refuse to trust me, in spite of all they have seen me do! I shall destroy them all!"

Moses pleaded with God for mercy; and God listened to Moses. God spared the people's lives. But He decreed that, except for Joshua and Caleb, not one of those who had set out from Egypt should enter the Promised Land. Only their children should do so.

So Moses himself, perhaps because of his own lack of trust, never entered the Promised Land. But he saw it; for before he died God told him to climb Mount Nebo, and there look across the lovely land of Canaan spread out below.

Moses appointed Joshua, the brave and faithful spy, to be the new leader (Deuteronomy 31: 1, 2, 7–8, 23–26; 34).

Was Joshua a good leader?

Yes. Joshua was a good leader because God was with him. Moses told Joshua, "The Lord, He it is that goes before you . . . He will not fail you . . . Fear not, neither be dismayed . . ." (Deuteronomy 31: 8). Joshua was full of wisdom because Moses, too, had blessed him (Deuteronomy 34: 9). And Joshua led the people into the Promised Land.

Why was a king first appointed?

The Israelites wanted a king, as other nations had. They thought a king would treat them more fairly than Samuel's sons, who ruled them as their present judges (1 Samuel 8: 4).

God directed Samuel to anoint Saul as their first king. Saul was tall, young and handsome. He was of the tribe of Benjamin; and he was utterly amazed

28

when Samuel told him he was to be anointed as king. "But I come from the smallest tribe in Israel!" he cried. "And my family is of no importance, even in our small tribe!"

Samuel invited Saul to dine with him. Afterwards, they sat on the roof of Samuel's house in the cool of the evening. There they spoke together.

Next day Samuel anointed Saul's head with oil, in the ceremony used by kings throughout the years. And Samuel told Saul other signs by which Saul could know he really *was* the man chosen by God to be King of Israel.

Even so, when the time came for him to be shown to the Israelites, Saul ran away and hid! God told the people where he was hiding; and they brought him out. "Long live the King!" they shouted. Samuel explained the powers of a king, and what rules should be kept. He wrote everything down so that there could be no misunderstanding. So Saul began to rule over the nation (1 Samuel 9; 10: 24, 25; 12).

Who was the next king?

At first Saul ruled well, keeping God's laws. But after a while he grew proud, doing as *he* wanted, making excuses to Samuel. Samuel warned Saul that if he went on in this way his kingdom would not last long; and sure enough, God finally said, "I no longer want Saul to be king. Go to Bethlehem, to the house of Jesse. I have chosen one of his sons to be the next king. You must go and anoint the boy."

The boy whom God had chosen was David – the David who was a shepherd boy, and who killed Goliath (1 Samuel 13: 13,14; 16: 1, 11–13; 17: 1–52).

Who were the founders of the twelve tribes of Israel?

Each tribe was named after and descended from one of the sons of Jacob. Their names are given below. Do you know what the symbols represent? Genesis 49 will help you identify them.

REUBEN

LEVI

SIMEON

JUDAH

ZEBULUN

ISSACHAR

DAN

GAD

ASHER

NAPHTALI

BENJAMIN

JOSEPH

What did a prophet do?

Prophets didn't look into the future like clairvoyants, as we might expect from our use of the word prophesy today.

First God spoke to the prophet, giving him a message for the people. It was then the duty of the prophet to pass on God's message, no matter what it was. They often had to be very brave. For instance, after the prophet Elijah had given an unwelcome message to King Ahab, he was in fear of his life. He had to escape quickly to a safe hiding place told to him by God (1 Kings 17: 1–6).

Who were the Levites?

At first the Levites were just one of the twelve tribes of Israel. There was nothing out of the ordinary about them. But when the tribes worshipped the golden calf, Moses called, "Whoever is for God, come to me!" All the Levites came to him, and obeyed the command to defend God's honour. From then on they were set apart as being God's special tribe.

The Levites now had the task of carrying out all the religious duties. God commanded that only men aged between twenty-five and fifty be allowed to take full part in the work at the tabernacle. When they were fifty they were to retire from regular service, although they could assist if they were needed (Numbers 8: 13–16, 20–26).

The Levites didn't have time now to earn their own living; so the people supported them by giving them a tenth of their own harvests and cattle, counting it as giving to God.

Who were the priests?

Moses' brother Aaron and his descendants were chosen for the special position of priests.

What were the duties of the priests and Levites?

Many of the duties were connected with the temple and the tabernacle. While the Israelites were in the wilderness the Levites actually carried the tabernacle and all its furnishings.

Another important duty was to teach the people God's law.

Only the priests were allowed to make sacrifices on behalf of the people. They also blew the silver trumpets of the Israelites.

There was a code of distinctive blasts for these trumpets, understood by everyone. Following God's command, the trumpets were used to call the people to meet together; sounded on festival and feast days; sounded when sacrifices were made to God; and sounded in battle (Numbers 10: 1–10).

And when the Israelites marched round and round the walls of Jericho before attacking it, and Joshua cried, "Shout! The Lord God has given you the city!" the trumpets blown by the priests sounded even before the war-cry of the people (Joshua 6).

People suspected of having the dreaded disease of leprosy had to show themselves to the priest. If the priest said it was indeed leprosy, the person was called 'unclean'. He or she had to live as an outcast. If they were cured, only the priests could declare them 'clean' again. This was why Jesus told the ten lepers who asked Him for healing to go and show themselves to the priest. When He spoke they still had the marks of leprosy on them. But they trusted Him enough to obey Him; and it was as they were on their way to find the priest they discovered their disease had been healed (Luke 17: 11–19).

What were the duties of the High Priest?

The High Priest was in charge of all the other priests. He also had some special duties.

Once a year, on the Day of Atonement, he alone was allowed to enter the Holy of Holies – the most holy place in the tabernacle.

Also, the High Priest was in charge of two sacred stones, called Urim and Thummim. He kept the stones in a pouch which he wore on his chest. When an important 'yes or no' decision had to be made, the High Priest would pull out a stone. The Thummim stone meant 'yes'. The Urim stone meant 'no'. The people believed that in this way God was directing them.

Who is sometimes called 'Our Great High Priest'?

This is the name given to Jesus (Hebrews 4: 14). Jesus' coming altered the need for all the old priestly rituals and sacrifices. Jesus Himself was the sacrifice for our sins on the cross.

34

Why was Jesus labelled 'The King of the Jews' at his Crucifixion?

It was the custom to label the cross on which a person was being crucified with the crime of which he had been found guilty. Pilate ordered that such a label be made for Jesus.

The label was written in Aramaic, Latin and Greek, so that everyone could understand it. But when the chief priests saw it they made an angry protest to Pilate. "It shouldn't read 'The King of the Jews'!" they cried. "It should say 'This man *claimed* He was King of the Jews'!"

But Pilate answered, "What I have written, I have written." And the label remained (John 19: 19–22).

People

What language did the people of the Bible speak?

Near the beginning of the Bible, after the flood, the Bible says 'And the whole earth was of one language, and one speech' (Genesis 11: 1).

But this didn't last. When the people decided to build a tower which would reach up to Heaven, God saw that they had grown so proud they thought they didn't need Him; so God made them all speak in different languages. They couldn't understand each other, and the building had to stop. The unfinished tower became known as the Tower of Babel, because in Hebrew, 'Babel' meant 'confusion'.

After a while people met up with others who spoke the same language. These groups got together and moved away from the rest. So the people were scattered over all the earth, each with their own language (Genesis 11: 2–8).

Why did the Israelites go to live in Egypt?

There was a famine in their own land, and Jacob's family (the Israelites) were starving. But there was corn in Egypt.

Years earlier Joseph, one of Jacob's sons, had been sold as a slave by his older brothers, and taken to Egypt. But Joseph still trusted God, and God watched over him as he grew to be a man.

When the Egyptian Pharaoh was troubled by dreams, God told Joseph their meaning. So Joseph was able to interpret them to Pharaoh. The dreams meant that Egypt would have seven years of good harvests, followed by seven years when the harvests would fail. The solution was to store grain in the good years.

Joseph was put in charge of seeing that this was done, and he carried out his task faithfully (Genesis 41: 28–49, 53–57). So the Israelites moved to Egypt to get food. They lived there for many years.

Were the Egyptians friendly to the Israelites?

At first the Egyptians were friendly. But as the years passed and the Israelites grew in number, they began to be cruelly treated.

If you read the book of Exodus, from chapter 2 to chapter 14, you will discover how God rescued them from Egypt by sending so many plagues on the Egyptians that the Pharaoh of that time finally agreed to let them go. (But even then he chased after them.)

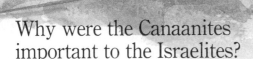

Why were the Canaanites important to the Israelites?

The Canaanites occupied the land of Canaan, a rich and fertile land. The Canaanites were the main group of people in Palestine at that time. Their towns were like fortresses, built on hilltops, with walls around them.

But they didn't worship God. Theirs was a 'nature' religion, and they had their own gods. The most important of these was Baal, the storm god. They believed that the rainfall – so essential to their harvests – depended on him.

God promised Canaan to the Israelites. He told Joshua how to capture its capital city of Jericho. A

huge procession of Israelites was to march round the walls of Jericho for seven days. On the seventh day they were to march round it seven times.

Then, at a signal from Joshua, the priests were to blow the trumpets of rams' horns, and the people were to give a mighty shout.

The Israelites obeyed. On the shout the walls of Jericho fell flat; and the Israelites swarmed into the city.

However, the Israelites never did occupy the whole land of Canaan. Some Canaanites remained there, especially in the place now called Lebanon, the coastal region to the north-west.

Who were the Philistines?

The Philistines lived to the south-west of Israel. For years there were constant battles between the Philistines and the Israelites because both wanted to possess the same land. King David finally defeated the Philistines, although the Philistines continued trying to claim new land for themselves whenever they could. The name 'Palestine' is derived from 'Philistine'.

Who were the Assyrians?

The Assyrians come into the Bible stories during the time of the prophets Amos, Hosea and Isaiah. They were a rich people, and their land was very fertile. Other nations were envious. The Assyrians often fought to guard or extend their frontiers; so they became known as a very war-like people.

Thousands of Assyrian clay tablets with writing on them have been found – including a whole library, collected by the Assyrian King Ashurbanipal.

Who were the Babylonians?

The Babylonians lived in what is now the southern part of Iraq. Clay tablets have been found there which were written over three thousand years before Jesus was born, showing their way of life.

Belshazzar was a Babylonian king. One day as he sat feasting in his palace he saw a hand, writing on the wall. He was terrified.

The words said that God had judged Belshazzar's deeds, and found them unworthy; so his kingdom would fall, and be divided amongst his enemies the Medes and the Persians. This did indeed happen, the very same night (Daniel 5).

Where do the Persians come into the Bible story?

The Persians, under King Cyrus, conquered Babylon. On God's command, Israelites who had been captive there were allowed to return home. They were also allowed to take back the treasures which belonged to the temple in Jerusalem, and to rebuild it (Ezra 1; 3; 4; 5; 6 and Nehemiah 1; 2; 3; 4; 6; 8).

Which part of the Bible often mentions the Greeks?

Greeks are often mentioned in the New Testament. Sometimes the word only means Gentiles (people other than Jews). But Paul spoke and wrote Greek; and much of his preaching was carried out in the Greek towns of Asia Minor – now known as Turkey.

Which people held power in the time of Jesus?

While He was on earth, Jesus lived in Palestine. The Romans ruled there at that time. They were a world power. They had become strong partly by conquering other nations, and partly by making alliances with them.

Were the Jews happy to be ruled by the Romans?

The Jews were very *unhappy*, although there were some good things about it. The Romans were extremely good at organization, and at building.

At first they tried to rule by using the Jewish kings. When this didn't work, they sent in Roman governors (procurators). The governors (including Pontius Pilate) found it hard to understand the Jews, and ruled them harshly.

For many years, even before the Romans, the Jews had been ruled by foreign powers, such as the Assyrians and the Babylonians. Now they were longing for a Messiah – a Saviour – to set them free. Many people expected the Messiah to defeat the Romans in battle and drive them out of the country. Because that expectation was so strong these people didn't understand Jesus' teaching of a new Kingdom. Jesus taught not of an *earthly* Kingdom, but of God's Kingdom of love.

Who were the Phoenicians?

The Phoenicians were the people who remained in their own part of Canaan even after most of that land had been occupied by the Israelites. One of their cities, Byblos, was probably where the alphabet was invented. When the Greeks took this alphabet to use themselves, they used the word 'biblos' to mean 'book'.

The Phoenician ports of Tyre and Sidon are often mentioned in the Bible. Cedar wood and purple dye were their main exports; but almost the whole of Ezekiel 27 is a list of the goods which passed through Tyre.

King Solomon gave King Hiram of Tyre twenty towns in Galilee because Hiram supplied the specially fine wood, gold and skilled craftsmen needed to rebuild the temple and palaces in Jerusalem (1 Kings 9: 10, 11).

In the New Testament, Mark says that people from the region of Tyre and Sidon were among the crowds who came to see Jesus (Mark 3: 8).

Why should we specially remember the Arameans?

The Arameans (or Syrians, in some Bible translations) were an inland tribe. They spoke Aramaic. This became a common language over a wide region, and was the language spoken by Jesus. The Aramaic word 'abba' means 'father' or 'dad', and is the word Jesus used in the Lord's Prayer when He said 'Our Father, Who art in Heaven'.

Who were the Scythians?

The Scythians (Ashkenaz) came from the north, riding strong, fast horses. The Bible says that in attack they came like a swarm of locusts, and the galloping horses' hooves sounded like the roaring of the sea. The Scythians cut through opposition – like a scythe (Jeremiah 50: 42; 51: 27).

Who were the Midianites?

The Midianites lived along the coast of the Red Sea. When Moses killed an Egyptian task-master he fled to Midian to hide from the Pharaoh's anger. As he sat resting by a well in the desert of Sinai, seven Midianite girls came to draw water for their flocks.

Moses watched idly, until some shepherds came along, roughly telling the girls to get out of the way until *their* sheep had had enough to drink. This wasn't fair! Angrily, Moses made the men wait. He drew the water for the surprised and delighted girls himself.

Their father Jethro invited Moses to stay; and after a while Moses married Jethro's daughter, Zipporah.

Animals

Which animals were kept by people of the Bible?

The Bible people kept sheep, cattle, goats, asses, camels, and (from King David's time onwards) horses, which were imported from Egypt and Assyria.

Why did they keep so many?

In very early times a man's wealth was measured by the number of possessions he owned, including his servants and animals.

Job was known as a very rich man. He owned seven thousand sheep, three thousand camels, one thousand head of cattle and five hundred donkeys (Job 1: 3)!

Before coins were minted, people would buy and sell goods by exchanging, or bartering, cattle.

In the Bible you will find many references to these animals. Here are some of the verses you might like to look at:
Genesis 32: 14, 15; Exodus 26: 7; Hebrews 11: 37.

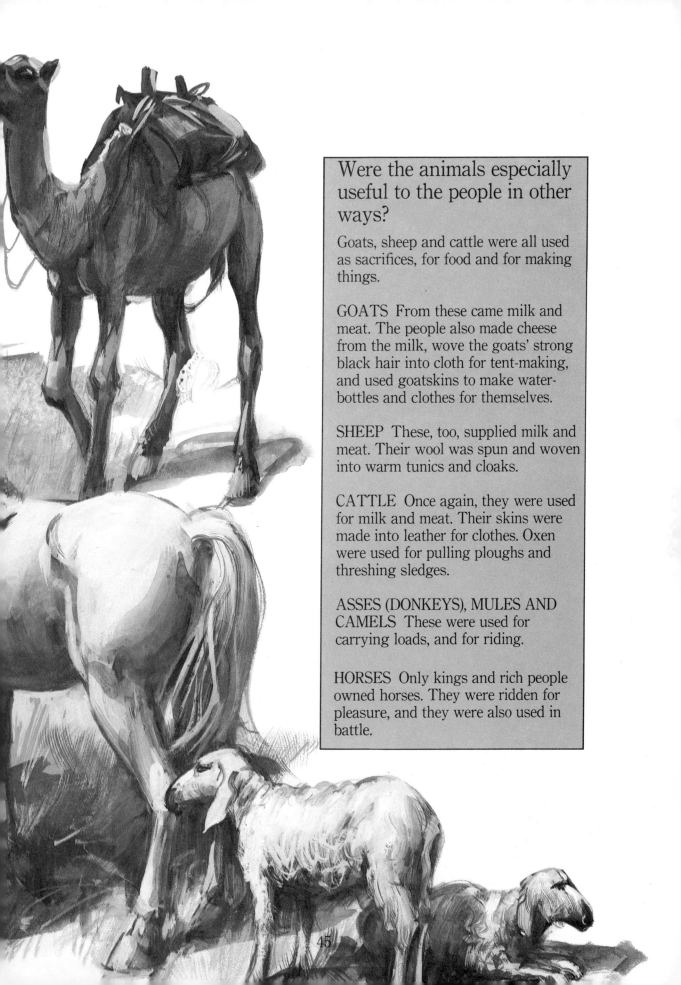

Were the animals especially useful to the people in other ways?

Goats, sheep and cattle were all used as sacrifices, for food and for making things.

GOATS From these came milk and meat. The people also made cheese from the milk, wove the goats' strong black hair into cloth for tent-making, and used goatskins to make water-bottles and clothes for themselves.

SHEEP These, too, supplied milk and meat. Their wool was spun and woven into warm tunics and cloaks.

CATTLE Once again, they were used for milk and meat. Their skins were made into leather for clothes. Oxen were used for pulling ploughs and threshing sledges.

ASSES (DONKEYS), MULES AND CAMELS These were used for carrying loads, and for riding.

HORSES Only kings and rich people owned horses. They were ridden for pleasure, and they were also used in battle.

What was an animal sacrifice?

An animal sacrifice was when an animal was killed and offered to God.

Why did the people of the Old Testament sacrifice animals to God?

They did this for various reasons. One was that they wanted to give the best they had to God.

They made sacrifices when they wanted to say 'thank you'. Noah did this when he and his family came safely out of the Ark after the great flood (Genesis 8: 20).

They made sacrifices to show they were grateful to God for His love and care, as Abel did in the story of Cain and Abel (Genesis 4: 4).

They made sacrifices when they wanted to ask God for forgiveness, and to help them, as David did when the plague was destroying the men of Israel (Genesis 21: 1–28).

But Samuel said to Saul, "God would rather you obeyed Him than made these sacrifices and burnt offerings!" (1 Samuel, 15: 32).

Jesus Himself was sacrificed, on the cross, when He was punished for the wrong things we have done so that we could be forgiven.

From then on, people no longer needed to sacrifice animals to God.

Where does the expression 'scapegoat' come from?

A 'scapegoat' is a person who takes the blame for another's wrong doing. On the most solemn day of the whole year, the Day of Atonement, the High Priest would make a sacrifice because of wrong things the whole nation of Israel had done. The sacrifice would be to 'atone' for the sins, or make up for them.

The High Priest would bring two goats to the tabernacle. He would cast lots to see which goat should be killed. The other, 'the scapegoat', would be kept alive and sent into the wilderness to escape, as a symbol of taking sin away, out of the presence of God (Leviticus 16: 7–10).

Did the Bible people keep animals as pets?

Every family which could afford it would buy at least two lambs at the time of the Feast of the Passover. One was killed and eaten as part of the celebrations, but the other would be kept as a pet. It would be brought up with the children, and sometimes even be allowed to drink out of their cups! As it grew old enough, it would be sheared and its wool used to make clothes for the family (2 Samuel 12: 1–3).

Why was the lamb so important in Israel's history?

The lamb was often used as a sacrifice. Later, Jesus was called the Lamb of God because He, too, was to be sacrificed (John 1: 29).

Was Jesus likened to any other animal?

Jesus was once called 'lion of the tribe of Judah', because the lion stood for strength, courage and power (Revelation 5: 5).

What did Jesus mean when He said He was the Good Shepherd?

Jesus may have been thinking of Psalm 23, where David talks about the Lord being his shepherd.

Jesus meant that He loves and cares for people, in the way that a good shepherd cares for his sheep. If they follow Him they need never be afraid (Psalm 23; John 10: 14). The symbol of the good shepherd was a very powerful one for the people because much of their time was spent looking after animals.

Which wild animals are mentioned in the Bible?

LIONS AND BEARS These could be dangerous to both people and animals. Shepherds had to watch their flocks very carefully, or the lambs might be seized and eaten (1 Samuel 17: 34).

Kings hunted lions, and also kept them in pits, or dens. People who had displeased the king would be thrown in, to be torn to pieces.

Samson once killed a lion; and passing it later found that a swarm of bees had settled in its dead body. He made up a riddle: "Out of the eater came forth meat, and out of the strong came forth sweetness." If you look up the story in the Bible, you'll be able to find out whether or not anyone solved the riddle (Judges 14: 12–17)! (Or perhaps you could ask your parents or teachers if *they* can solve it.)

Daniel was thrown into a den of lions because he refused to stop worshipping God, and worship King Darius instead; but God kept Daniel safe and unharmed (Daniel 6).

Lions were hunted to such an extent that by New Testament times it was rare to see a wild lion in Israel.

Two Syrian brown bears once attacked a crowd of young men who were making fun of the prophet Elisha. The bears mauled 42 of the mob (2 Kings 2: 23, 24)!

Syrian brown bears still live in the Middle East, although they have disappeared from Israel itself.

FOXES These small animals like fruit, and often damage the low grape vines which grow in Israel. Jesus must have watched the little foxes, seeing them on their lone hunting expeditions, and noticing their lairs. Once He said, "The foxes have holes, and the birds of the air have nests; but the Son of Man (Himself) has nowhere to lay His head," (Matthew 8: 20).

JACKALS Jackals lived and hunted in packs, searching for their food at night. Although in the story of Samson, it says he caught 300 foxes, it's much more likely that they were jackals (Judges 15: 4).

LEOPARDS Leopards were well known to the Israelites of Bible times. They are mentioned both by Isaiah and Jeremiah. Isaiah looks forward to the day when the leopard won't kill even a goat; and Jeremiah asks whether the leopard can change his spots (Isaiah 11: 6, Jeremiah 13: 23).

WOLVES Wolves were thought to be very fierce because they killed sheep and lambs for food. Jesus told His followers to be careful of people who came to them pretending to be as innocent as sheep, but were really as dangerous as wolves (Matthew 7: 15).

DEER Fallow deer, roe deer, antelopes, gazelles and ibex were all found in Bible lands. They are often mentioned in the Bible.

Were the Bible people allowed to eat any kind of animal?

Some animals were called 'clean', and some 'unclean'. The Israelites were allowed to eat the 'clean' animals, and there were rules explaining which was which. The rules applied to birds and fish as well as mammals (Deuteronomy 14: 3–21).

Were there any very large creatures in Bible times?

Isaiah talks about a leviathan – a huge, gliding, coiling, sea serpent (Isaiah 27: 1).

In Job, God describes a behemoth. It ate grass, but it was immensely strong. Its tail swung backwards and forwards like a cedar tree in the wind. Its limbs were like rods of iron. It used to lie under the lotus trees, hidden amongst the reeds in the marsh; and it wasn't afraid even when the river Jordan raged (Job 40: 13–23).

Some people think the behemoth was a dinosaur.

Are many birds mentioned in the Bible?

There are eagles, vultures, kites, falcons, ravens, horned owls, screech owls, hawks, little owls, great owls, white owls, desert owls, osprey, cormorants, storks, herons and hoopoes. There are also bats.

Did Jesus like animals?

We can be sure He loved them as part of God's creation. Also He spoke about them, and once said that although sparrows were sold very, very cheaply, not one of them fell to the ground without God knowing (Matthew 10: 29).

Food

What did people of the Bible lands eat?

The people ate mainly cereals, fruit and vegetables. They also ate fish, and there were pistachio nuts and almonds. The rich people ate meat: lamb, veal and beef; but the poor people would only have meat on a special occasion. Butter was sometimes made, although it didn't keep well in the hot climate. Cheese and yoghurt were eaten, and by the time Jesus was born many people kept hens, so were able to have eggs.

When did people start to grow crops?

People grew crops almost from the beginning of Bible times. Adam and Eve's son Cain 'tilled' or worked the soil (Genesis 4: 2).

Which crops did they grow?

They grew barley and wheat, peas, beans, lentils, onions, leeks, melons and cucumbers. They also grew grape vines. Later on, many people had their own olive trees. Figs were picked from the trees and date palms were cultivated. Citrus fruits were just beginning to be known in the New Testament.

Unless the crops grew, the people starved. Famines were common. One famine, in the time of Joseph, lasted for seven years (Genesis 41: 30, 43: 1, 47: 13).

In fact the crops were *so* important that attacking enemies would strike during the growing season, and destroy them.

Did the people know how to make bread?

Yes. Barley bread was the most common, although wheat was also used. Poor people were allowed into the fields at harvest time to glean, or 'pick up', any grain which the reapers left behind (Ruth 2: 3).

Was bread important to them?

Yes. Bread was the main part of their diet. It was so important they also used the word 'bread' when they meant 'all our food', as Jesus did when He prayed 'Give us this day our daily bread' (Matthew 6: 11). He also called Himself 'the Bread of Life'.

Did they make their bread as we do today?

They had to make their bread by hand. It was women's work. First the women would grind the corn by rubbing it between two flat stones, or, later, between two millstones. Then they took the flour and mixed it with water or olive oil to make dough. Often there was no yeast to make the bread rise, so the women would knead in some fermented dough which they had saved from the previous baking. The fermented dough was called leaven. Then the bread was baked, not in the shape we usually see today, but flat.

What methods did they use to bake the bread?

There were several ways of baking bread.

One method was to make a shallow hole in the ground and light a fire in it. By the time the fire died down the hole would have become very hot. Then the ashes would be scraped out, and the flat rounds of dough placed against the sides of the hole to bake.

Sometimes a shallow, flat-bottomed bowl made of clay would be placed over the fire, and the dough laid on top of the bowl.

Or stones might be put into the fire. When they were hot enough the stones would be raked out, and the dough laid on them to cook.

Richer homes would use ovens made of clay. Before the Romans, the oven would simply have had one compartment, with the fire at the bottom and the dough placed around the sides near the top.

By the time of the Romans these ovens had two compartments, one above the other. The floor between the compartments had holes cut into it, so that when a fire was lit in the lower part the heat would rise into the upper part. The dough would be placed around the walls of this upper part.

Sometimes the ovens were buried in the ground, to keep the heat in.

Did they have any special customs connected with bread?

Yes. One was that the bread must never be cut, only broken. The loaves were made so that this was easily possible. Even today people in some churches talk about 'The Breaking of Bread' when they mean the service of Holy Communion, the service in memory of the Last Supper, when Jesus broke the bread and gave it to His disciples (Matthew 26: 26).

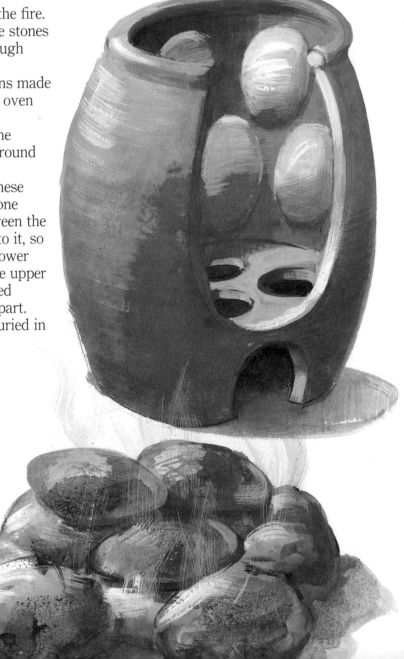

Did they cook other food?

For special occasions they cooked cakes and pastries. They also cooked meat and fish, and made vegetable stews.

Apart from the baking of bread, cakes and pastries the most usual method of cooking was boiling in a pot over a fire.

Since water was often very scarce the people used oil, both for boiling and poaching.

Fish might be dried and salted so that it would keep, and then eaten with bread when required. Or it might be cooked over an open fire and eaten at once.

What were the food laws?

The people of the Old Testament had very strict laws about food. The Israelites were allowed to eat only fish which had fins and scales. They weren't allowed to eat shellfish, for example. And the animals which they ate for meat had to be mainly those which chew the cud *and* have divided hooves. Nothing connected with a pig might be eaten, because although it has a divided hoof it doesn't chew the cud. Nor must a camel be eaten, because while it chews the cud it doesn't have a split hoof (Leviticus 11: 4, 7).

Where did salt come from?

Salt was obtained from the Mediterranean and the Dead Sea. Water would be poured into large pans. When it had evaporated in the sun, salt would be left. There were also salt mines.

To eat salt together is still a sign of friendship among Arabs. And at first 'salary' meant the money given to a Roman soldier so that he could buy salt.

Did the people have sugar?

No. They mainly used honey from wild bees to sweeten their food (Judges 14: 8). They might also have made a sweet syrup by boiling up locust beans and dates.

What did they drink?

The water from a local well, or a clear stream, was usually safe. The people also drank milk from the family goat and wine made from grapes.

Why did Jesus choose bread and wine for His Last Supper?

Bread and wine would always have been included in the evening meal. But at the Last Supper Jesus said the bread, broken for the disciples to eat, represented His body which was to be broken for them on the cross; and the wine represented His blood, which was

Are there any stories in the Bible about food?

Food is often mentioned, but in some of the stories it is especially important, for example, when God sent quails and manna from Heaven to feed the Israelites in the desert (Exodus 16), when Elijah was fed by ravens (1 Kings 17: 2–6), and when a boy gave his five loaves and two fishes to Jesus in the feeding of the five thousand (Matthew 14: 13–21).

There is also the story of Jesus cooking fish to make breakfast on the shore for His disciples, after His resurrection (John 21: 13).

to be shed for them. The blood was a sign of the new covenant, or agreement, which His followers would have with God.

Today, bread and wine is taken at Holy Communion in remembrance of this, as Jesus asked (Luke 22: 19, 20).

Festivals

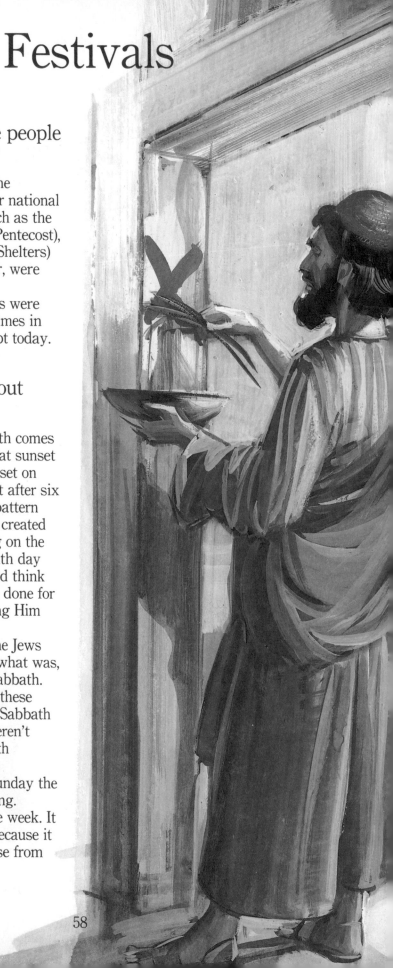

What festivals did the people of the Bible celebrate?

They had festivals to mark the important happenings in their national life. Some of the festivals, such as the Feast of Weeks (later called Pentecost), the Feast of Tabernacles (or Shelters) and the Feast of the Passover, were more important than others.

Most of the Jewish festivals were celebrated from the earliest times in their history, and are still kept today.

What do we know about these festivals?

THE SABBATH The Sabbath comes every seventh day. It begins at sunset on Friday and lasts until sunset on Saturday, and is a day of rest after six days of work. This was the pattern established by God when He created the world in six days, resting on the seventh. God made the seventh day holy; a day when people could think about Him, and what He had done for them, and be happy in serving Him (Genesis 2: 2, 3).

But by the time of Jesus the Jews had made many laws about what was, or was *not*, allowed on the Sabbath. Jesus showed people that all these laws weren't necessary. The Sabbath was made for them. They weren't made just to keep the Sabbath (Matthew 12: 1–14).

Today some people call Sunday the Sabbath day; but this is wrong. Sunday is the first day of the week. It is celebrated by Christians because it is the day on which Jesus rose from the dead.

THE FEAST OF THE PASSOVER
AND UNLEAVENED BREAD This
Feast comes in March or April, the
first months of the Jewish religious
year. It is a movable feast, that is, as
happens with Easter for Christians, it
is not held on the same date each year.

Passover celebrates the time when
the Israelites fled from being slaves in
Egypt. The Pharaoh would not let
them go free, so God sent nine plagues
on the Egyptians. The last plague was
the death of every first-born Egyptian
child. To make sure the homes of the
Israelites were spared from this
sorrow, God instructed that a lamb or
young goat should be sacrificed for
each family. The meat would be eaten
and if the door posts of the homes
were marked with the blood of the
lamb the Angel of Death would pass
by – hence 'passover'.

God also commanded that the
festival be celebrated by all the
generations of Jews yet to be born, to
give thanks to Him for the escape from
slavery and the safe journey to the
Promised Land.

What is eaten at the Passover feast?

As God commanded, for the seven
days of the feast, unleavened bread is
eaten – bread made quickly, without
yeast. This reminds people that in the
haste of getting away from Egypt that
was the only bread there was time to
make.

Bitter herbs are also part of the
meal. The herbs remind people of the
years of sadness and suffering in the
wilderness. Wine is drunk, and with
every glass or cup a blessing is said,
saying that God is ruler of the
universe, and creator of the vine from
which the wine is made.

Do the children understand this?

Every year the children are told exactly why the festival is held, and what each item of food means (Exodus 12).

Do people celebrate the feast in their own homes?

To begin with, people always celebrated the Passover feast in their own homes; but by the time of the New Testament it was one of the festivals for which they would travel to Jerusalem.

Is the Passover connected with the crucifixion of Jesus, and Easter?

Jesus' crucifixion and resurrection took place at around the time of the Passover (Mark 14: 1, 2). So the early Christians, and Christians today, celebrate Easter at this time.

THE FIRST FRUITS This festival was held during the feast of Unleavened Bread. The first sheaf of corn from the harvest was presented to God by the priest, and reminded people of the first harvest that was reaped in the Promised Land.

THE FEAST OF WEEKS, LATER
CALLED PENTECOST The feast of
Weeks was celebrated at the end of the
grain harvest, fifty days after the
offering of the first sheaf of barley at
the First Fruits. The feast was later
called Pentecost because in Greek
'pentecost' means 'fiftieth'.

THE FEAST OF TABERNACLES, OR
SHELTERS This was a very happy
time. It was celebrated in the autumn,
and was a time of thanksgiving to God
for the fruit harvest.

The labourers worked very long
hours picking the grapes and olives, so
for the harvest weeks they lived in
shelters in the fields. The shelters were
made from tree branches, and saved
the people from a long daily walk to
and from their homes.

These 'tents' were known as
tabernacles, and reminded people of
the time when the Israelites had lived
in tents all the time.

THE FEAST OF TRUMPETS,
LATER CALLED NEW YEAR
A trumpet was blown on the first day
of every month (New Moon); but the
first day of the seventh month was
especially important. No regular work
was done on this day, so that the
people could gather together and make
special sacrifices to God (Numbers
29: 1–6). Later, the day was counted as
a religious New Year festival.

DAY OF ATONEMENT On the Day
of Atonement the High Priest made a
sacrifice to 'atone' or make up for the
wrongs done by the Nation of Israel.
You can read more about it in the
Animals section.

THE FESTIVAL OF LIGHTS
(HANNUKAH) This festival, also
known as 'Dedication' (John 10: 22),
was named 'Lights' because lamps
were specially lit in synagogues and
homes every evening. It celebrated the
restoration work done on the second
temple by Judas Maccabeus.

SABBATICAL YEAR God
commanded that every seventh year
the land must be allowed to rest, that
is, to lie fallow. During this year
anything which *did* grow on it was to
be food both for poor people and
animals (Exodus 23: 10, 11).

Besides this, every seventh year all
Israelite slaves were to be offered their
freedom (Exodus 21: 2–6). Also, debts
had to be cancelled. If this was done
willingly, God would specially bless
the person to whom the debt had been
owed (Deuteronomy 15: 1–11).

Did everyone in the Bible keep the same festivals?

No. For example, the Canaanites worshipped many gods. They believed they could influence these gods by using magic rituals. Instead of harvest festivals, they held Fertility Festivals.

There were three harvest festivals. Did the people have a special reason for celebrating harvests?

Although the farmers and labourers worked very hard they knew they couldn't control the east wind, and the drought which it brought. They realized they depended entirely on God for the rainfall, and the coming to life of the seeds which they had sown. Since without God there couldn't *be* a harvest, all the crops belonged to Him, and were holy. The people could only eat the corn and fruit after they had first offered it to God.

What did the prophets think about worshipping those gods?

You will be able to discover just how much the prophets disapproved if you find these verses in the Bible: Judges 2: 11; Jeremiah 11: 17; Jeremiah 32: 35; Hosea 9: 10; and Hosea 13: 1.

Clothes

What did rich people wear?

Rich people's clothes were similar in
style to poor people's; but the rich
would have clothes for working,
clothes for leisure time, clothes for
winter, and clothes for summer. A rich
man would also have various
lightweight coats to wear over his
tunics.

What were rich people's clothes made of?

Their clothes were mainly either of
wool or linen. The linen was made
from flax.

The Egyptians were able to make a
very soft linen, known in the Bible as
'fine' linen. Joseph wore a fine linen
robe when he was governor in Egypt
(Genesis 41: 42).

Camel hair was also sometimes used
for making coats.

Did all people of the Bible wear the same sort of clothes?

The clothes were mainly of the same style. Otherwise there were quite a lot of differences, depending on whether the people were rich or poor, and what material they were able to use. Priests wore special clothes, according to the law.

What did poor people wear?

A man would wear a loin cloth or a short skirt. Over this he would wear a simple calf-length tunic, fastened round the waist with a belt or girdle. If he needed to be able to move freely he would shorten his tunic by tucking it up into his belt, thus 'girding up his loins'. The prophet Elijah once tucked up his tunic in this way, and, because the power of God was with him, ran faster than a chariot and horses (1 Kings 18: 46)!

A man also wore a thick woollen cloak. This could be used as a blanket at night and, folded, as a cushion during the day. A poor man's cloak was very important to him. There was even a law about it. If a man owed money, he might hand over his cloak as a pledge that he would settle the debt. But his cloak had to be given back to him at sunset.

A woman's tunic would be longer than a man's, reaching down to her ankles. The tunic was often dyed blue, and would usually have the special pattern belonging to her village embroidered on its yoke.

What were poor people's clothes made from?

Poor people's clothes were usually made from wool or goats' hair, and they probably had only the one set.

Very poor people, and the prophets, often wore clothes made from the skins of animals. John the Baptist wore this kind of tunic when he was in the wilderness (Mark 1: 6).

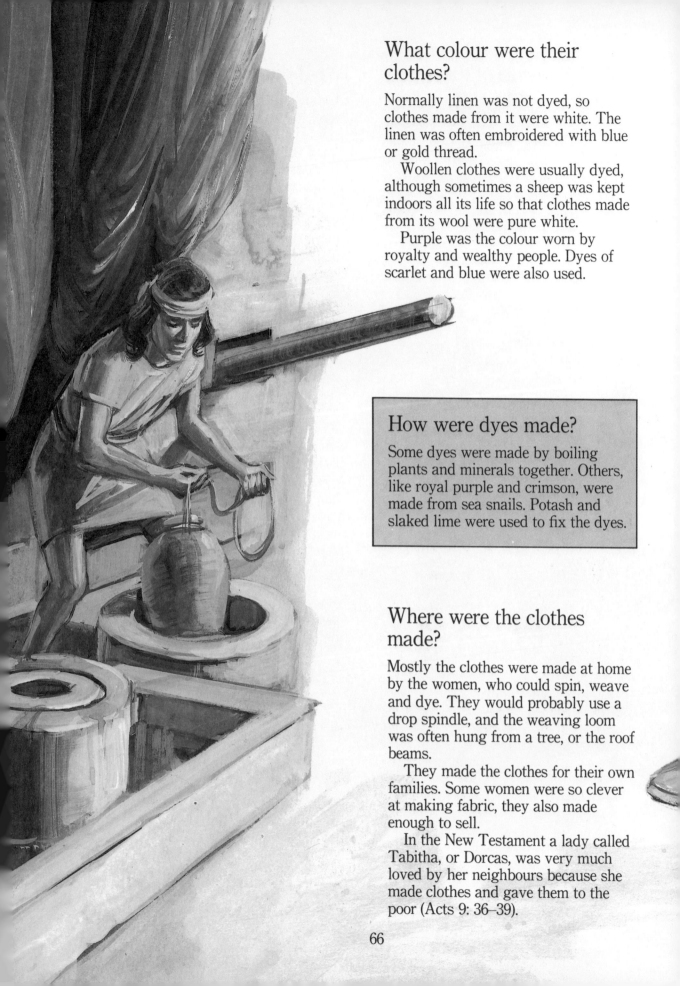

What colour were their clothes?

Normally linen was not dyed, so clothes made from it were white. The linen was often embroidered with blue or gold thread.

Woollen clothes were usually dyed, although sometimes a sheep was kept indoors all its life so that clothes made from its wool were pure white.

Purple was the colour worn by royalty and wealthy people. Dyes of scarlet and blue were also used.

How were dyes made?

Some dyes were made by boiling plants and minerals together. Others, like royal purple and crimson, were made from sea snails. Potash and slaked lime were used to fix the dyes.

Where were the clothes made?

Mostly the clothes were made at home by the women, who could spin, weave and dye. They would probably use a drop spindle, and the weaving loom was often hung from a tree, or the roof beams.

They made the clothes for their own families. Some women were so clever at making fabric, they also made enough to sell.

In the New Testament a lady called Tabitha, or Dorcas, was very much loved by her neighbours because she made clothes and gave them to the poor (Acts 9: 36–39).

What did people wear on their feet?

Outdoors people normally wore sandals. Indoors they went barefoot. The sandals were always taken off before going into a Holy place, or into another person's home. It was the custom to take off the right sandal first, and then afterwards to put it on first.

People's feet got very dusty on the hot, dry roads. It was the job of the most humble servant in the household to meet visitors in the doorway, take off their sandals, and wash their feet. Yet Jesus washed His disciples' feet, at the Last Supper (John 13: 5).

Did people ever go barefoot out-of-doors?

They went barefoot if they were very poor, or if they were fasting.

Did people wear hats?

They wore headdresses to protect them from the heat in summer, and cold winds in winter.

Did they have nightclothes?

No. When they lay down to sleep they loosened the clothes which they had worn during the day.

What was special about the coat Jesus wore?

It was woven from top to bottom without a seam (John 19: 23).

What was sackcloth?

Sackcloth was woven from goats' hair and camel hair. It was very uncomfortable to wear. People put it on when they wanted to show God they were sorry about wrong things which had been done.

Daniel wore sackcloth and ashes when he was praying to God for forgiveness for Jerusalem (Daniel 9).

What was special about Joseph's coat?

It was a coat of many colours, which his father gave to him (Genesis 37: 3). His brothers were very jealous of the coat.

Did Jesus think that the more grandly a person was dressed, the more important the person was?

No. Jesus knew that clothes were not important. He once said that the lilies of the field were clothed more splendidly than King Solomon (Luke 12: 27), and He told the scribes and Pharisees they were more interested in their appearance than in doing God's will (Matthew 23: 5).

What did important soldiers wear for battle?

They were protected by heavy armour, made of bronze, as the giant Goliath was (1 Samuel 17: 4–7).

Homes

Did the Bible people live in houses?

Many of them did. But some of the Bible people were nomads, that is, they weren't settled in one spot but moved from place to place. The nomads lived in tents. Obeying God's words, Abraham, with his family and servants, left his home in the city of Ur to live a nomadic life (Genesis 12: 1–5).

What were the tents made from?

They were made from goats' hair. When the goats had been sheared, the hair was woven on a loom. This made a strong material, striped in black and brown.

How was the tent made?

A long length of cloth was selected.
Wooden rings were sewn down the
middle and along the edge. The tent
was then propped up, using poles and
guy ropes, and the family lived in the
space underneath it.

One part of the tent was closed off
at the back with a divider made either
from twigs and reeds woven together,
or more goats' hair cloth. This part
was divided in two. One section was
curtained off completely for the women
to use. The stores were also kept in
that section. Only the male head of the
family was allowed to go into the
women's section. The other section had
an open side, like a porch, for visitors.

The floor was usually just bare earth,
although sometimes woven matting
was used.

The hard work of putting up the
tent was always done by the women.

Which important person in the New Testament was a tent-maker?

Saul, later called Paul, was a tent-
maker. All Jewish males were
supposed to learn a trade. Usually
their father taught them. Paul was
careful to earn his own living as he
travelled and preached the Gospel
(1 Thessalonians 2: 9).

What were the houses made of?

The houses had foundations of rock. The walls were made of rough stones or bricks. If the houses were being built in an area where rocks were scarce, the foundations might also be of bricks.

How were the bricks made?

A hole was dug in the ground. The hole was filled with chopped-up straw, pieces of charcoal, palm fibre, pieces of shell, and water. This mixture was trampled on with bare feet until it became a soft mud which could be worked.

The bricks were either laid out to dry in the sun, or baked in kilns.

The Israelites toiled hard, making hundreds of these bricks when they were slaves in Egypt (Exodus 5: 10–12).

Some of these bricks lasted more than three thousand years, like the ones at Tell el-Kheleifah (Ezion-geber) the 'city-of-bricks-with-straw'.

Rulers often commanded that their royal mark should be inscribed on the bricks. Some of these bricks still exist. Perhaps you may be able to see them in a museum, or find pictures of them in a library book.

Archaeologists have made many very interesting discoveries about buildings in the Bible lands. For instance, they have found remains of the houses built in the city of Ur at the time of Abraham. You might like to see if you can find out about other discoveries. Perhaps your parents or teachers might help.

What was used for mortar?

Mud or slime was used to cement the bricks together. In long periods of wet weather the houses leaked, or even dissolved! Also, a thief could easily make a hole in the wall.

How were the rooves made?

The rooves were flat. Beams of wood were laid widthways across the tops of the walls. Other beams were then laid over them, making a criss-cross. The roof was filled in with layers of earth, clay and brushwood, and rolled with a stone roller to make it firm. Or matting covered with plaster might be used.

It was quite easy to make a hole in the roof, as the four men did when they brought the man who couldn't walk to Jesus (Mark 2: 1–4).

Were the rooves specially important to the people?

The roof was almost like an extra room. In the cool of the evening the family would climb up on to the roof to sit. They would reach the roof by using a ladder if they were poor, or steps if they had been able to afford to have them built. In very hot weather the family might even make a tent of branches, and sleep up there.

While they were on the roof, people

74

would often shout their news across to the family next door, who would be on their own roof. News would be passed from roof to roof, which is how the saying 'shouting the news from the roof-tops' arose.

When it had been raining, grass often grew on the roof, and the smaller animals belonging to the family might be put up there to graze!

When the sun shone, fruit and grain were spread out on the roof to dry. A lady called Rahab even hid some spies under the flax which was drying on her roof (Joshua 2: 6).

Weren't people worried about falling off the roof?

There must have been some accidents of this sort, because a law was made that when a new house was built the roof must have a parapet, or low wall, round the edge. Then, if someone did fall and was killed, the householder wouldn't be held to blame (Deuteronomy 22: 8).

What were the houses of the rich like?

The houses were large. They had two storeys. The rooms were built around courtyards and gardens. This meant there was always some shade, bringing cooler air into the house even in the heat of the summer.

In winter the rooms which had most sunlight could be used.

Later, rich people even had bathrooms. These were just tubs set into the floors.

The houses were furnished simply, with matting on the floor, seats, small tables, and bedding. They were lit by oil lamps.

What were the houses of the poor like?

The house had one room, with a yard outside. The windows were small, and as high up in the wall as possible. This helped to keep the room cooler in summer, and warmer in winter. There was no glass, but the windows had shutters.

The room was divided into two parts by a low platform, constructed in the area furthest from the door. The family lived on the platform. Probably the space under it was used for storing things. Bedding, cooking things and clothes were kept on the platform.

The area nearest to the door had a floor of beaten earth. During the cold weather, or if thieves were suspected of being about, the animals were brought into the house at night, and this was their space.

There was also a hole dug in the earthen floor for the fire. There was no chimney, and the room must have been very smoky. In the summer there were lots of insects everywhere.

The room was very dark. There was always an oil lamp, kept on a shelf furthest away from the light from the door.

Jesus knew about this kind of house very well. He lived in one just like it, in Nazareth. And when He told the story of the woman who lost her coin, He knew she would have to light the lamp before she could search for it (Luke 15: 8).

Were the houses comfortable?

From the time of Solomon the houses of the rich people were very comfortable. The houses of the poor were possibly not a lot more comfortable than tents.

How many people lived in the same house?

Whole families – parents, grandparents, children, aunts and uncles often lived together in the same house; and they were always ready to offer hospitality to visitors. Space was very cramped. But as soon as the family could afford it, it was fairly simple to build on an extra room.

How big were the towns and cities?

At first the twelve tribes of Israel settled in small farming communities, or villages. Many of the villages gradually developed into towns of between 150 and 200 houses. Later, especially about the time of Solomon, towns became larger. The towns always had walls built round them, for protection against attack.

Later still, towns and cities began to be planned, rather than allowed to grow haphazardly.

At the time of Jesus there were probably a quarter of a million people living in the city of Jerusalem.

Travel

Was travel easy in Bible times?

Moving from place to place was difficult, and could often be dangerous. Much of the danger came from bandits, who lay in wait for travellers, to attack and rob them.

Jesus knew well about this danger. He once told a story about a man who had been attacked by robbers as he walked from Jerusalem to Jericho. The man was left lying by the roadside. First a priest, then a Levite, came along; but they passed by on the other side of the road. A Samaritan (a man from Samaria) stopped to help the poor man, lifting him on to his donkey, taking him to an inn, leaving him in the care of the innkeeper, and even paying the bill (Luke 10: 25–37).

We still call people 'good Samaritans' today when they do something to help others.

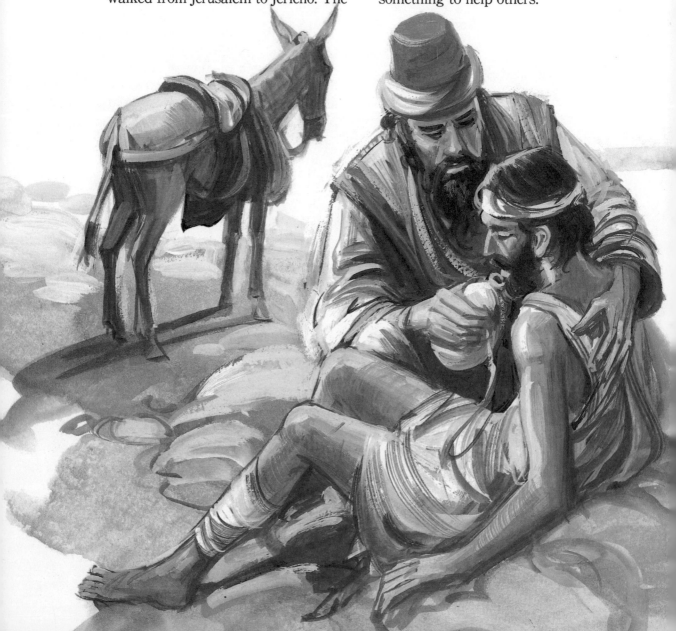

Why did people in the Bible travel?

People travelled for many reasons.

One of the most important was trade. There were established trade routes by land and sea.

When people found they couldn't make or grow *everything* they needed themselves, trading – buying, selling, or exchanging – began.

At first this was simple, and mainly local. But as market-places grew up near the gates of towns and cities, merchants began to travel around, setting up stalls to sell their goods, then moving on to the next place.

Joseph's brothers sold him as a slave to some travelling merchants. The merchants took him to Egypt, to sell him in the market-place there (Genesis 37: 25).

Nomads (tent-dwellers) kept huge numbers of grazing animals. When all the food in one place had been used up, the nomads travelled on to find fresh pastures for their flocks.

If the crops where they lived failed, people had to travel in search of food for themselves. For instance, when there was famine in Canaan, Joseph's brothers went to Egypt to buy corn – little expecting to find Joseph there (Genesis 42)!

When the Egyptian Pharaoh made the Israelites work as slaves they moved on for two reasons: to escape from their slavery, and because God commanded them to. They wandered in the desert for 40 years, on their way to the Promised Land (Exodus 13: 17; 17: 1; Numbers 14: 34).

When a ruler wanted to count his people he would order a census to be held. This meant that the people had to travel to the place where they had been born, to be counted. This was why Joseph and Mary had to travel to Bethlehem, although they knew it was almost time for the birth of baby Jesus (Matthew 2: 1–6).

Jewish families travelled to Jerusalem to celebrate festivals. Jesus was taken to Jerusalem for the Feast of the Passover when He was twelve years old (Luke 2: 41, 42).

On foot, or even riding a donkey, the journey from Nazareth to Jerusalem would have taken several days. People travelled in groups to be safer from attack by bandits – which makes it understandable that Joseph and Mary could have set out on the return journey without realizing that Jesus wasn't with them. They decided to go back to Jerusalem, where they found Him in the Temple (Luke 2: 41–51).

How were most overland journeys made?

Ordinary people mostly travelled on foot. Even if the family owned a pack-donkey, some of the family would have to walk. The donkey, or ass, was the main beast of burden, and was domesticated long before the horse or the camel.

Moses and the Israelites travelled on foot through the desert for 40 years, on their journey to the Promised Land.

Jesus and His disciples usually walked from place to place. But as He entered Jerusalem on the first Palm Sunday – the Sunday before His death on the cross – Jesus rode on a donkey (Mark 11: 1–11). He did this to fulfil the Old Testament prophecy 'Behold, the King comes to thee, lowly, and riding upon an ass' (Zechariah 9: 9).

Traders usually travelled in a caravan – a convoy – of camels. In a group they were less likely to be attacked by bandits.

Camels were strong. They could each carry a weight of about 180 kilograms, and a rider. They could survive for two weeks without water, and could withstand the heat and the sandstorms. They could also provide milk for the travellers.

The caravan would have an experienced leader who knew the route well; but if by chance the way was lost, camels could even be killed and eaten so that the men could survive.

Horses were mainly used by armies. Horses were very expensive to buy and keep, and less useful as pack-animals than camels or asses.

Were there any wheeled vehicles?

For people who could afford it there were horse-drawn chariots, small two-wheeled carts, and four-wheeled wagons. The carts and wagons would be pulled by horses or oxen, and guided by a person walking in front. Some of the wagons were covered, and had curtains at the sides – but springs hadn't yet been invented. The roads were so uneven, the ride must have been very bumpy!

The man from Ethiopia was travelling in a chariot along the desert road from Jerusalem to Gaza when the apostle Philip was sent by God to speak to him. The chariot couldn't have been going very fast, for Philip was able to run beside it long enough to overhear the Ethiopian reading aloud from the book of Isaiah (Acts 8: 26–39).

What were the roads like?

In Old Testament times the roads were rough, bumpy tracks, easily turned to mud in the rain. Because the roads were so poor, travelling by cart or chariot was often no faster than walking.

When the Romans began to build their excellent roads, chariots and carriages came into more use. The roads had good foundations, with flat, paved stones on top. Sometimes these stones were specially cut. The roads were so well built, we can still see some of them today.

Nothing stopped the Roman roads! Rivers were bridged, causeways were constructed over marshy land, rocks were tunnelled through.

The Roman roads went directly from Rome to the provinces of their Empire. This is where the saying 'all roads lead to Rome' comes from.

However, the roads only went where the Romans wanted them to go and there were still many journeys which had to be made on the old unpaved roads.

Were there any pavements?

In towns the streets were very dirty. The Romans built raised pavements so that pedestrians could avoid the dust and mud.

Was it safe to travel by sea?

The Mediterranean was reasonably safe during the summer, but in wintertime ships only sailed across it in an emergency. Ships could sail from port to port along the coastline; but even this was dangerous.

What were the ships like?

The ships were built of wood. They were sailing ships, relying on wind power, with the additional use of oars; and were possibly not very seaworthy, since they often sank. The ships were used for carrying cargo, but passengers were sometimes taken.

Who owned the ships?

Some merchants bought ships of their own. Others had to hire one. If they had to borrow money for this it was always lent at a very high interest rate. So many ships sank, with the loss of cargo and crew, the money couldn't always be repaid.

Which person in the Bible made many journeys by sea?

The apostle Paul travelled by land and sea on his missionary journeys – and was ship-wrecked three times!

Acts chapter 27 tells about one of Paul's voyages in great detail. Paul was being sent as a prisoner to Rome. He advised the ship's captain that setting sail from Crete late in the year was unwise; but the captain wouldn't listen. As the ship sailed across the Adriatic it was caught in a tremendous storm. Everyone gave up hope of being saved. Then Paul spoke, telling them an angel of God had come to him, saying he must reach Rome in safety. No one would be drowned. Only the ship would be lost.

The ship *was* wrecked; but Paul and the crew swam ashore, and found they had landed on the island of Malta.

Who else in the Old Testament thought he would drown?

Jonah was commanded by God to go and tell the people of Nineveh that their city was to be destroyed because of their wickedness. Afraid to deliver such a message, Jonah caught a ship going in the opposite direction, to Tarshish.

The ship set sail. But a tremendous storm blew up. "Pray to your God to save us!" the captain begged Jonah.

Shouting above the noise of wind and waves Jonah answered, "This has happened because I was trying to run away from God. Throw me overboard! Then the sea will be calm."

Seeing there was no other way, the terrified crew obeyed. At once the storm died away. Jonah thought he must drown. But God sent a huge fish, which swallowed Jonah in one gulp, coughing him up on to a beach three days later!

At last Jonah was ready to obey God's command to go to Nineveh. To his surprise, far from being angry and disbelieving, the people repented; and Nineveh was saved from destruction.

Did people use the rivers for travel?

Only the Nile, the Euphrates and the Tigris were really suitable for navigation. The main use was for trade. Sail barges were used on the river Nile, bringing corn down to the port at its mouth.

Crafts

Did the people of the Bible have jobs?

In Bible times there were no factories or offices and some of the jobs which would today be done by 'professionals' or 'skilled craftsmen' were done by each household, probably because 'trade secrets' were passed down from father to son.

Jesus' father, Joseph, was a skilled carpenter. In Bible days, apart from working on buildings, carpenters made yokes, ploughs, threshing boards, carts, tables and other furniture.

Jesus Himself would have made these things in the carpenter's shop at Nazareth. Perhaps He was thinking of His days there when, trying to explain to the listening people how much He wanted to help them, He said, "Take My yoke upon you . . . for My yoke is easy, and My burden is light" (Matthew 11: 29).

We must also remember, of course, that a lot of jobs we do today would not have been possible in Bible times – like being a computer programmer or a professional footballer!

Was building very skilled work?

Not all of it, especially in the beginning. People laboured by themselves or in communities to build houses, dig wells, dig cisterns for storing water, dig water tunnels, and build walls round cities. Stones were rough hewn.

During the time of David and Solomon skills began to develop. The masons and carpenters sent by King Hiram to help in building the Temple passed on their crafts to the Israelites. Corners of buildings began to be jointed and bonded. To give extra strength to the walls the technique of laying stones both widthwise and lengthwise (stretchers and headers) was used. The stones themselves were finely shaped, and put together so skilfully no mortar was needed.

Later, the Israelites gained knowledge of building construction from the Persians, Greeks and Romans.

How did the people of the Bible make pottery?

A potter needed clay, which was dug from the earth, and a supply of water, usually from a stream or a cistern. He also needed a potter's wheel on which to shape the clay, and a kiln in which to bake, or 'fire', his finished pots.

First the clay was left outside so that the sun, rain and frost would break it up, and impurities be washed away. If the potter intended to make cooking pots, he might at this stage mix ground limestone into the clay so that the finished pots would be able to withstand heat. He then had to fire the pots at a lower temperature, or the limestone would decompose.

Mostly, however, the potter simply used raw clay. Adding the water was a skilled task. It had to be measured out and poured on evenly. All the air had to be squeezed out of the mixture, otherwise the pots would be imperfect. The clay would have bubbles in it, and the pots might crack when they were fired.

The clay and water mixture was trampled on until it became mud. Isaiah talks about 'one who comes from the north' treading on the rulers of the nation as if he were a potter treading on clay (Isaiah 41: 25).

Once the clay was ready, the potter would normally use his potter's wheel to shape it into pots. The pots were left to dry out. Often they would then be put back on the wheel again, and shaped more delicately.

Sometimes the pots would be roughly made by unskilled workers, and later shaped by the skilled potters.

Were there other methods of shaping the clay?

Sometimes the clay would be pressed into a mould. In New Testament times clay lamps were usually made in this way.

The clay could also be modelled freely. The Israelites made toys from freely modelled clay.

What objects were made from pottery?

Household ovens; all kinds of bowls; oil lamps; jars for storing wine, water or oil and for keeping documents safely; water-bottles for carrying on a journey; tiny jugs for perfume; objects such as weights for looms; objects connected with religion; and toys such as horses and camels: all were made from clay pottery. Dolls were also made from clay, but it's not certain whether these were toys, or used in some forms of religion.

Was it easy to fire the pottery?

Firing the pottery was a very skilled task. The kiln had to be at just the right temperature for the type of clay being used, and the length of time of the firing had to be carefully judged.

Was the pottery decorated?

Sometimes the Israelites 'burnished' their pots. This was done at the drying stage. Selected parts of the pot were rubbed by a tool made from wood, stone or bone. When the pot came out of the kiln later, the burnished areas would shine.

The Israelites sometimes painted a line of red or black around a water jar or jug; or they might decorate objects with a 'slip'. A slip was done using a special kind of clay which had iron in it. The clay was mixed with water and brushed on to the pot to produce the pattern.

Were toys made?

As well as horses, dolls and camels, children in the Bible had tiny bowls and furniture made from pottery.

Ancient Egyptian children had pull-along toys made of wood, and balls made from painted cloth. They also had spinning-tops, made from wood, and marbles, which they rolled through a wooden board with three arches cut into it. The aim was to knock over the skittles standing behind the board.

There were also board games such as chess and draughts. The boards were made from stone, ebony, ivory or,

once again, clay. A form of Ludo was also known.

The die was either a disc, with two sides, or a teetotum – a pyramid with four sides.

Did they make jewellery?

Jewellery was made from gold, silver and semi-precious stones like cornelian, rock-crystal, jasper and agate. The stones were cut and polished.

Where did the gold come from?

The gold came from gold mines.

The Israelites had to import gold, as well as silver, tin and lead. The only metals in Israel's mines were iron and copper.

King Solomon had a fleet of trading ships which returned to port every three years carrying gold, silver and ivory (1 Kings 10: 22). When Solomon was building his temple, Hiram's ships brought him gold from Ophir (1 Kings 10: 11).

How were gold and silver worked?

The metal was melted and poured into moulds. When the Israelites wanted to make themselves a god to worship, Aaron collected up all their gold earrings, melted them, and poured the molten gold into a mould in the shape of a bull (Exodus 32: 4).

Sometimes the gold was beaten into sheets. Objects were overlaid – covered – with gold. In Solomon's Temple the altar was made from cedar wood overlaid with gold. The cherubim were made from olive wood overlaid with gold. Even the walls were overlaid in this way (1 Kings 6: 20–28).

In the Temple in Jerusalem, apart from the other items, the spikes to keep birds off the roof were made of gold!

What were copper and iron used for?

Iron was used to make weapons –
arrow-heads, spear-tips, lances, swords
and daggers.

Tools such as axes, chisels and
plough points were made from copper
or iron, as were needles, safety-pins,
bracelets and tweezers.

Copper or iron bowls and
pails were also made.

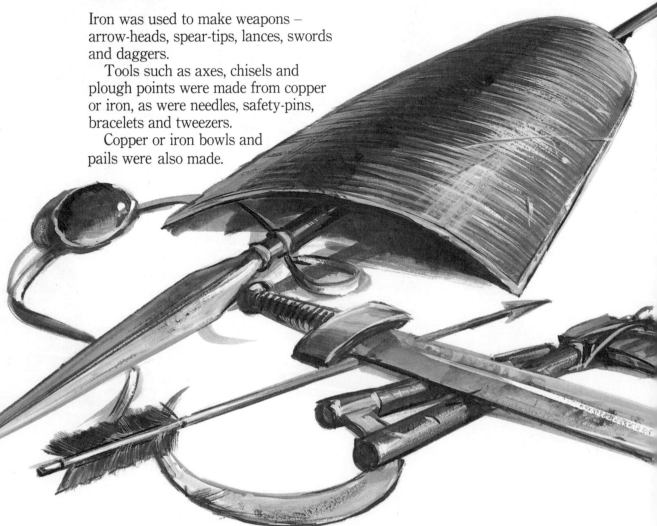

What were coins made of?

Early coins were made from an alloy
of gold and silver called electrum.
These were minted in Lydia around
eight hundred years before Jesus was
born. Each coin was a piece of metal
stamped with its weight, to guarantee
its value.

The weights were standard, and
coins often became known by the
name of their weight. For example,
'shekel' first meant a weight, then a
coin.

Coins were later made from single
metals – gold, silver, bronze, copper or
brass. In the beginning copper was
shaped into discs, and silver was
weighed into pieces which could be
carried around easily in a bag.

How were copper and iron worked?

The blacksmiths melted the metal in a furnace, in a pot made from clay. They could then shape it as they wanted. Sometimes they poured the molten metal into moulds made from stone.

Working with iron was difficult, as it had to be kept hot all the time it was being shaped.

When the army of Saul and Jonathan was preparing to fight the Philistines there was not one blacksmith in the land. The Philistines had forbidden the defeated Israelites to have blacksmiths, in case they made weapons. On the day of the battle only Saul and Jonathan possessed a sword and a spear. Even to get their tools sharpened or mended the Israelites had to take them to the Philistines, who charged enormous prices for the job (1 Samuel 13: 19–22).

How were musical instruments made?

The Israelites had string, percussion and wind instruments. We don't know how all of them were made, but stringed instruments such as the harp and the lyre had wooden frames. The lyre was plucked with the fingers, but a plectrum may have been used when playing the harp.

Cymbals were made from copper, and tambourines or timbrels from wood and painted animal skins.

Pipes were hollow, made from cane, bone or wood, with finger-holes bored at the correct intervals. These pipes had a reed in them.

Horns or cornets were made from the horns of animals, often a ram's horn.

Leather, silver, gold, gut, ivory and shell were also used in the making of instruments.

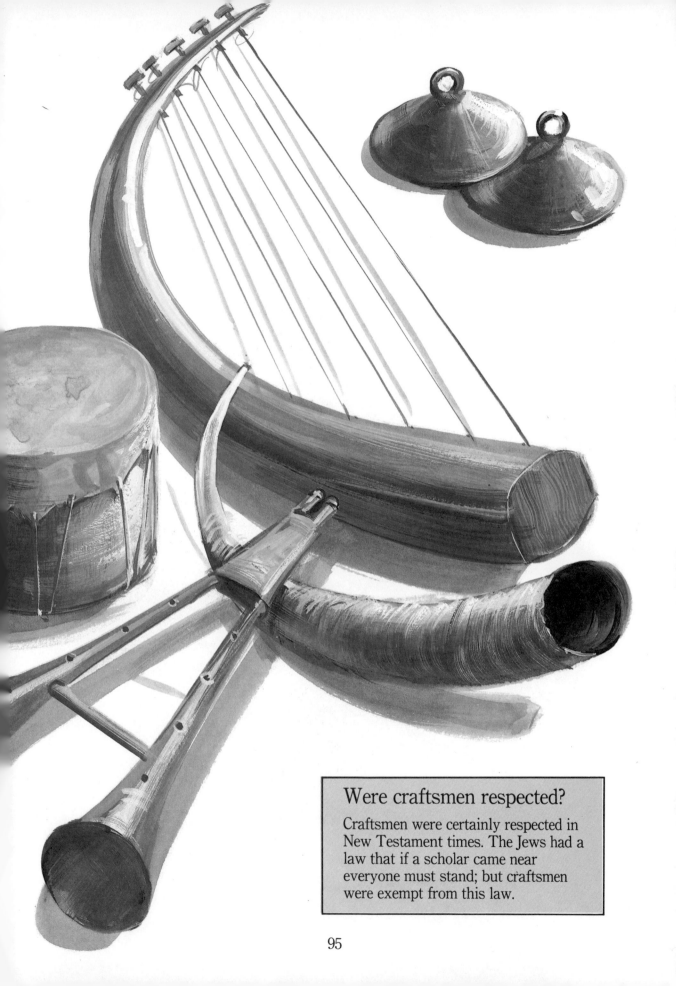

Were craftsmen respected?

Craftsmen were certainly respected in New Testament times. The Jews had a law that if a scholar came near everyone must stand; but craftsmen were exempt from this law.